CONTENTS

FOREWORD

Halley's Comet holds a very special place in astronomy for several reasons. It is one of the brightest comets that visits our galaxy, and it is visible for a relatively short period, so, when it does make one of its visits to the neighbourhood of the Sun, professional and amateur astronomers alike have a good chance to see it. Of course, much of the importance of this comet stems from Halley's observations of the comet when it appeared in 1682. He brought together much of the previous work on comets, and he laid the basis for all the work to come on these celestial bodies.

As our knowledge of the dimensions of the Solar System, our Galaxy and the rest of the universe change, we have to keep up–dating our ideas about the place of comets in astronomy. Many of these changes have been brought about by new, exciting advances in technology. First naked eye instruments, then telescopes, and, more recently, spectroscopes and cameras, have played a part in adding to our understanding.

This visit, however, marks the first time that the techniques of space science have been applied to the study of Halley's Comet. Judging from the discoveries made by space probes visiting the planets, we can expect the Halley's Comet probes to yield some real surprises!

I hope this book will help you discover something new for yourself, and perhaps set you on the path to learn even more about astronomy.

Percy Seymour

David

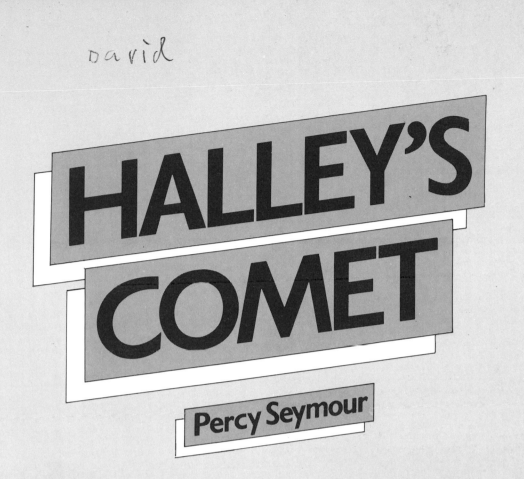

HALLEY'S COMET

Percy Seymour

DRAGON
Granada Publishing

Dragon Books
Granada Publishing Ltd
8 Grafton Street, London W1X 3LA

Published by Dragon Books 1985

Seymour Percy
    Halley's comet
    1. Halley's comet – Juvenile literature
    I. Title
    523.6'4   QB723.H2

ISBN 0-583-30864-3

Designed and produced by Dave Allen & Associates

Editorial Consultant: Felicia Law

Printed and bound in Great Britain by Purnell

Colour reproduction by Regency Graphics, Bath

Typeset by David Gilmour Associates

A ONCE-IN-A-LIFETIME EVENT

The State of Texas in the USA is well-known today as the home of rich oil-men, sophisticated businessmen, and the space technology centre at Houston. So it's probably difficult to believe that in the nearby city of Dallas, in the year of 1910, there was a brisk trade in "comet pills". These were supposed to ward off the evil influence of a comet that was due to pass close to the earth that very year. The comet, as you may have guessed, was Halley's Comet, and its appearance sparked off the most surprising alarm.

Right from the earliest times, it seems that these fascinating visitors to our skies have been accused of causing catastrophies. They were said to be warnings sent from the gods, so naturally, whenever they appeared they made a lot of people feel very uncomfortable. In 44 BC, for example, a comet blazed across the sky, and the famous Roman dictator Julius Caesar was assassinated. In AD 1066 a comet lit the skies, and sure enough, England was conquered by William of Normandy who was to be known from then on as William the Conqueror. In fact the Bayeux Tapestry, which tells the story of the invasion, includes a scene showing the comet very clearly above the head of the unfortunate King Harold. We now know, of course, that the comet in the picture is none other than Halley's comet making one of its earlier visits.

Comets are just one of the many physical phenomena that occur in the universe and they have been observed by humans for a long time. In the past when phenomena could not be explained easily, people gave them supernatural or mysterious meaning. In many cases this superstition led to even greater misunderstandings, and sometimes, even to

King Harold looks unstable on his throne, while his courtiers "are in awe at the star" – (Isti Mirant Stella).

panic or fear. An eclipse of the sun, for example, was regarded with terror as a sign of doom and destruction.

Finding out about things in a logical, precise or scientific way has not only helped us to learn a wealth of things about our universe, but has put an end to the kind of fear and misunderstanding that prompted people to buy "comet pills". The return of Comet Halley in 1986 gives us a once in a lifetime chance to observe and find out more about this truly fascinating phenomenon. We shouldn't miss the opportunity.

HERE IT COMES...

Comet Halley orbits the sun on an average about once every 76 years. The closest point that any orbiting body comes to the sun is called its perihelion, and Comet Halley's last perihelion date was April 20th 1910. Using the knowledge gained by Edmond Halley, after whom the

Latitude 20^{0}N – 77^{0}N

Equator

Latitude
18^{0}N – 32^{0}N

November 1985

December

January 1986

February

6

comet is named, and using modern scientific techniques and equipment, astronomers can predict that the comet will reach its next perihelion on February 9th 1986. However the comet will be visible long before and after that date, especially if viewed through a large telescope.

As early as 1982 two astronomers called Danielson and Jewitt began to look for the returning comet. They thought then that it would be close enough to be picked up by the world's second largest telescope, the 508 centimetre (200 inch) Hale reflector at Palomar Observatory in the USA. Sure enough, their calculations proved correct and a tiny speck was visible on their computer screens just where they thought it should be.

From that date until now, Comet Halley has been growing brighter and brighter as it approaches the sun. However, only between November 1985 and May 1986 will it be visible to the naked eye or through binoculars. So, it is this time period that is important to us.

Below is a diagram that will show you when the comet is easiest for you to observe. Those of you in the Southern Hemisphere will have the opportunity to see it at its very brightest.

Equator

Latitude 20°S – 70°S

Equator

February

March

April

May

COMETS:PART OF OUR SOLAR SYSTEM?

Our solar system is generally thought to have evolved about 4,600 million years ago. It began as a huge cloud of gas and dust. At some point the dust fragments were so squeezed and compressed together that they began to exert a gravitational pull on each other. The result was a ball of gas and dust under great pressure. Eventually nuclear reactions began, resulting in the glowing ball that we call our sun.

Around the infant sun there hung a disc made up of leftover gas and dust debris. Over a period of millions of years, these particles of dust collided and stuck together. The clumps grew and grew in size, until they formed what we now call the planets. Much of the gas drifted into space but some of it was held by the gravity of the planets and now forms their atmospheres.

THE SOLAR FAMILY

We divide the solar system, (sol is the Latin name for sun) into two distinct parts: the inner half, which is made up of the small planets Mercury, Venus, Earth and Mars; and the outer half, made up of the large, mostly gaseous planets, Jupiter, Saturn, Uranus and Neptune. Between Mars and Jupiter lies the mass of rocks and rubble known as the asteroid belt. And, of course, many of the planets have smaller bodies, which we call moons, orbiting around them. Pluto lies at the outer edge of the solar system and seems to be composed entirely of methane gas.

Pluto

Neptune

Uranus

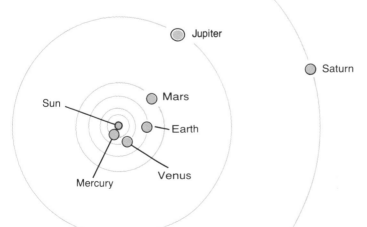

Jupiter

Saturn

Mars

Sun

Earth

Mercury

Venus

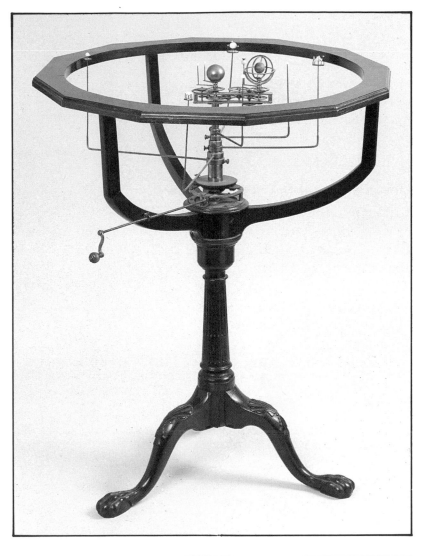

An orrery is a mechanical model of the solar system. The various planets move manually or by clockwork around the Sun.

COMETARY CLOUDS

When we think of the solar system we usually think of the sun, its planets and their moons. However, it is probable that another group of bodies was also formed when the solar system first came into being and that this group now forms a kind of cloud with the sun at its centre. The cloud is called a cometary cloud and it is made up of thousands of millions of comets all orbiting the sun, but with orbits which lie beyond the edge of our planetary system.

In 1950, the Dutch astronomer Jan Oort, working at the University of Leiden, first suggested the idea that comets were stored in a huge cloud that moved around the sun. He estimated that the cloud stretched out as far as 50,000 astronomical units, that is 50,000 times 149,597,870 km (92,975,676 miles)! Today the cloud bears his name. It is called Oort's cloud.

Some people have a different theory to explain how Oort's cloud was formed. They think that possibly the cloud was made up of interstellar dust which was collected by the sun as it made its way along its own orbit within our galaxy. This theory would mean that the planets and the comets were formed differently, even though they have many similarities.

OUR GALAXY

At the centre of our solar system is the sun, and the sun is a star just like the ones you see twinkling brightly or dimly in the night sky. It is one of about 100 thousand million stars that make up our galaxy, which we often call by the more familiar name of the Milky Way.

The Milky Way is shaped like a disc with curved arms flowing outwards at the edges. The sun and our solar system lie about 30,000 light years from the centre (in one of the spiral arms). On a clear night we can look inwards towards the dense mass of stars that makes up the centre of our galaxy. It was this band of "starlight" that first came to be known as the Milky Way.

Dense star clouds in Sagittarius are seen from Earth looking towards the centre of the Milky Way.
(Photo: R. Royer S.P.L., London)

Nucleus

Our galaxy, the Milky Way, rotates on its axis, so that all the millions of bodies scattered throughout it, are rotating on orbits of different distances and speeds. The sun takes about 250 million years to complete one journey around the centre of the galaxy so it is always on the move. Throughout this journey it runs into some of the many gas clouds that are strewn about the galaxy and in doing so may pick up some of the cloud's gas and dust debris. This, as you already know, is how some scientists think Oort's Cloud, the cloud of comets, was created.

Beyond our galaxy there are more galaxies. In fact the universe seems full of them and more are being discovered all the time as observation techniques improve. There seem to be three basic types. There are spiral galaxies like our own, barred spirals which have a bar of stars through the middle, elliptical galaxies which look much like lenses in space, and irregular galaxies which, as their name suggests, can take many different shapes.

There are also such things as radio galaxies, which give out very strong radio waves and quasars which are very far away and may be young galaxies in the early stages of their formation.

Particles spiral around the magnetic lines that thread their way through the spiral arms of the Milky Way.

WHAT IS IT MADE OF?

Early observers could easily describe the shape of a comet as it passed through the heavens, but they had little idea of what it was made of. Today we can use very sophisticated methods like 'spectroscopy' to help us solve the mystery. As you may know light is made up of a "spectrum" or band of colours which range from violet to red. It also contains colours that we cannot normally see like ultra violet, and infra red. Different chemicals absorb light in different ways and so their spectral bands are specific to them just as a fingerprint is specific to each person. The analysis of spectra is called spectroscopy and we can use it to analyse the spectrum of light that comes from a comet and so discover its chemical composition.

THE DIRTY SNOWBALL

We now know that at the very centre of each comet there is an irregular shaped clump of water–ice and dust. This may measure anything from a few hundred metres from centre to edge to a few tens of kilometres depending on the comet's size. We call this the nucleus.

When the comet is a long way from the sun, say over 5 astronomical units (5 A.U.), the nucleus simply absorbs the sun's energy and keeps itself warm. In this state we would not be able to see it. But when it comes closer to the sun, the surface begins to get very warm. It gets so warm in fact, that the surface ice turns into water vapour, or gas. This causes a spherical cloud of vapour and dust to form around the nucleus and this we call the coma. When the ice turns to vapour it releases other chemical substances, such as ammonia, which are themselves heated and turned into gas. They become part of the coma as well. The coma and the nucleus together are called the head of the comet and it is the head which glows so brightly in the sky. The coma may stretch from 10,000 km (6,215 miles) to almost 1 million km (62,150,504 miles) out into space.

GAS AND DUST TRAILS

The flow of gas from the nucleus will pull dust particles with it. The sun's radiation, in turn, will blow the particles away from the nucleus in a direction away from the sun. The dust trails backwards for up to 10 million km (621,504,000 miles)

tail

nucleus

coma

12

from the comet head and is seen as a beautiful curving tail. Astronomers call it a Type II or Type III tail.

A Type I or plasma tail is not made up of dust but of gas molecules from the mixture of gases found in the coma. It is very long and straight and is swept away from the head of the comet by a stream of gases ejected from the sun. This stream is known as the solar wind. It is the force of the solar wind that makes the plasma tail straight and not curved like the dust tail.

Most bodies in space rotate on an axis. The earth, as you know, rotates once every 24 hours. Comets also rotate. When a particular part of the surface of a comet faces the sun it may give off an extra spurt of gas. This shows itself as a halo in the coma. Astronomers can measure the exact period of rotation of the comet by watching the spacing between haloes.

A section of a page on cometary observation from 'Astronomicum Caesarium': Petrus Apianus. Printed 1540. By courtesy of the Royal Astronomical Society. The position of the comet's trail in relation to the sun has been accurately studied.

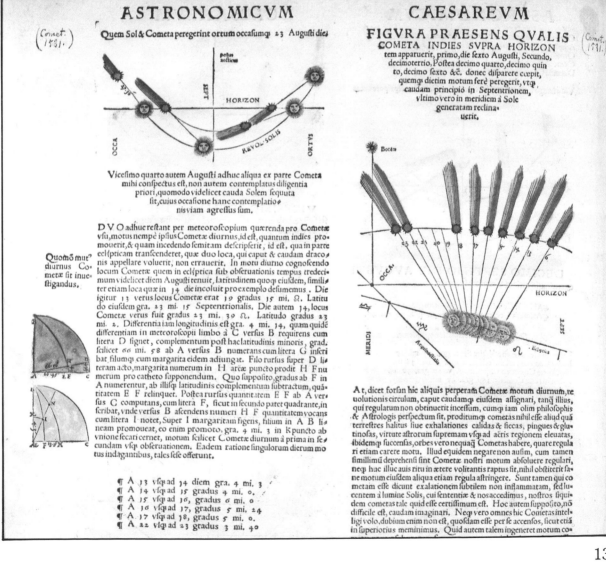

COMETS THROUGH THE AGES

As we have learned, there are probably thousands upon thousands of comets travelling in independent orbits through the galaxy. However, only a tiny percentage of these enter our solar system, and become visible in our skies.

From the very earliest times, astronomers and mathematicians have known that these passing "stars" did not fit into the fixed pattern of the solar system. Whether right or wrong, in their answers to the comet "riddle", they almost always advanced the science of astronomy by their work.

THE HAIRY STAR

The ancient Chinese were very interested in the sky and made quite detailed studies of it. They most certainly knew that comets existed, but they did not know what they were. The Ancient Greeks also recorded the activity of comets. It is from the Greek that we get the name comet. They called it 'aster kometus', the hairy star! Aristotle, the Greek philosopher, thought that they were bits of Earth's atmosphere that had caught fire! This seems a little far-fetched to us perhaps, but Aristotles' theory was accepted as the truth until well into the 13th century.

During the 16th century astronomers took a little more interest in comets. An Italian called Frascastoro observed that the tail of a comet changed direction, always pointing away from the sun. This meant there was some sort of relation between comet and sun. (See illustration on page 13).

The 'hairy star' as drawn in AD 648

PARALLAX EXPLAINED

In 1577 a Danish astronomer by the name of Tycho Brahe began to study a comet that had just appeared in the sky. He decided that he would establish its position in the sky in relation to the stars and planets.

Tycho used something called parallax to help him measure the distance between the earth and the comet. You can best understand parallax by doing a very simple experiment. Hold a pen in front of your face and note the objects in the background behind it. First close your left eye and look at the pen with your right eye. Don't move your

Tycho Brahe 1546 – 1601.

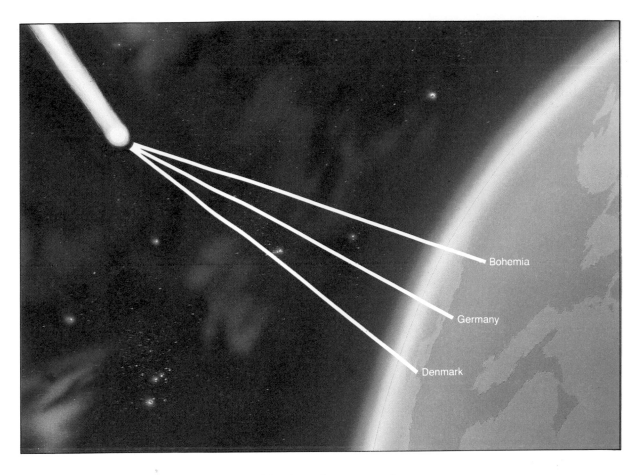

Calculating the parallax.

head. Now close your right eye and look at the pen with your left. You will see that the pen has shifted position in relation to the objects in the background. The amount of shift depends on how close, or far away, the pen is from your eyes. The further away the pen is the less the shift.

If something is very far away you need to observe it from two different places to see the parallax. If you calculate the amount of parallax and the distance apart of the two observation points you can calculate the distance away of the object itself.

Tycho Brahe reasoned that if the comet was within the Earth's atmosphere, the parallax would be much greater than that of the moon. To help him measure he used an astronomer in Germany and one in Bohemia. Both noted the position of the comet in relation to the stars behind it. Tycho made his own observations from Denmark. When he had collected all of the data he found that the comet remained in the same place no matter from where it was observed. The parallax was small, much smaller than that of the moon. His conclusion was that the comet was much further away than the moon. It was indeed a body and outside Earth's influence. Aristotle had been wrong!

Astronomy dates back so far into prehistoric times that we can only guess at its beginnings. The stone circle at Stonehenge in England, which was begun some 4,000 years ago, is a fine example of an early system built to monitor the movements of the sun and the moon. The circle was used mainly for religious worship. However some mathematical and scientific readings, probably in connection with the calendar, must also have been carried out there. Time, the calendar and astronomy have always had strong links.

Early Egyptian astronomers watched the progress of the moon, the planets and the stars very carefully as they travelled across the sky. They, too, were interested in time, and they used their observations to help create calendars.

However, it was not until the Greek civilization developed some 25 centuries after Stonehenge, that observers tried to reason out exactly where the sun, moon and stars were in relation to each other. An ancient astronomer called Aristarchus actually put forward the idea that the sun was at the centre of the solar system. Nobody took him seriously!

In AD 2 Ptolemy came up with a different theory. He said

WHAT IS AN ELLIPSE?

The shape of an ellipse is easy to draw with the following apparatus:
 a pencil
 a block of board approx. 30 cms (20 in) square
 2 drawing pins or tacks and a hammer
 a length of string about 24 cm (15 in) in length

WHAT TO DO:

1. Place the drawing pins or tacks firmly in the board about 10 cm (6 in) apart.
2. Knot the piece of string and loop it round the tacks. Place a pencil inside the looped string and pull until taut. Mark the board with the point of the pencil. Keeping the string taut around the pencil, continue to trace the ellipse shape onto the board, moving the pencil right round the tacks.

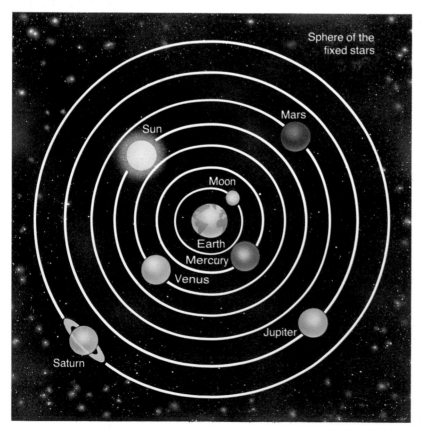

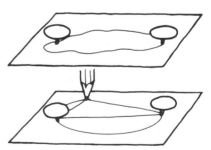

Ptolemy's plan of the solar system.

that the earth was at the centre of the system and that the sun and planets revolved around it. Because the theory suggested that our Earth was at the centre of everything and that mankind was therefore very important, the idea went unchallenged for 1,400 years.

Then in 1530, Nicolaus Copernicus bravely wrote an essay that once more suggested that the sun was the centre of the solar system. He proposed that the planets revolved around the sun, but still believed that they moved in epicycles. An epicycle is a circle the centre of which moves along a larger circle called a deferent.

Johannes Kepler, a German astronomer, agreed in part with Copernicus, but he did not believe that the orbits of the planets consisted of epicycles and deferents. Instead, he described them as ellipses. An ellipse is like a circle that has been pushed down so that it is flattened at the top and bottom. Kepler worked out the orbital paths of all the known planets, then turned his attention to comets! If they were heavenly bodies then they might also have orbits. Unfortunately, Kepler decided in the end that they did not. He believed that comets moved in a straight line across the sky, that they passed through our solar system and vanished for ever into space.

Nicolaus Copernicus 1463 – 1543.

Johannes Kepler 1571 – 1630.

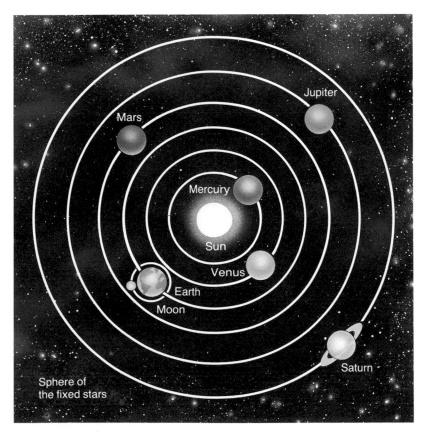

Copernicus' plan of the solar system.

17

COMETS: ELLIPTICAL JOURNEYS

It was an Italian astronomer by the name of Borelli who made the next step in discovering how comets moved. He disagreed with Kepler's straight line theory and said that although a comet approached the sun in what seemed to be a straight line, it then swung around the sun and sped off in the direction from which it had come.

Borelli studied the movement of a particular comet that appeared in the sky in 1664. He reckoned that the only way to explain its passage was to assume that its path followed a very elongated ellipse. Now an ellipse has two foci that are located on its horizontal axis. The longer the ellipse, the further apart the foci are. An orbital ellipse has the sun as one of its foci. Borelli thought that the ellipse along which his comet travelled must in fact be virtually open ended.

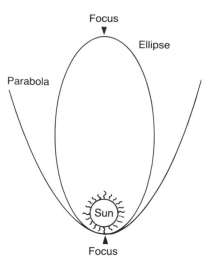

Cometary paths.

PARABOLIC PATHS

The first focus would be the sun but the second would be so far beyond the solar system that it could not be plotted. Such an open ended curve is called a parabola. He deduced that the path of the comet must therefore be a parabola, and that as with all the comets, its path would take it around the sun once, then swing it out and into space, never to be seen again.

Kepler's theory certainly accounted for the way in which planets moved around the sun. And Borelli went on to offer a more believable explanation of the way in which comets moved. Astronomical knowledge was growing quickly! However, no one as yet understood why they moved more quickly when passing close to the sun.

NEWTON AND GRAVITY

The man who studied these problems and found their solutions was the great scientist Isaac Newton. Newton was a brilliant mathematician and he was the first to really stress the importance of the concept of gravity or the way in which all bodies seemed to attract each other. During the years 1685 and 1686 he produced amongst other things a book which he called *Philosophiae Naturalis Principia Mathematica*. It is known today simply as *Principia* and it is one of the great landmarks in astronomy.

In his book Newton detailed his theory of universal

Isaac Newton 1642 – 1727.

gravitation. He proposed that *every* body in the universe attracts *every* other body. The strength of the attraction depends upon how much mass, or matter, each body contains, as well as their distance apart. Newton's equations could be used to calculate exact orbits and also to understand speed differences as bodies drew closer to each other. They could also be used to understand Borelli's theory about the parabola shaped orbit of comets.

Once it had been written, *Principia* needed to be published; and the man who suggested to Newton that he should write up his theories in the first place was a fellow scientist and friend of Newton — Edmond Halley.

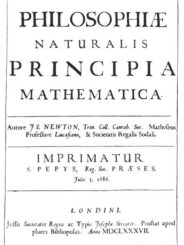

Three figures argue different ideas on comet orbits. Are they within Earth's atmosphere, do they pass on a straight line and vanish for ever, or do they originate near Jupiter and Saturn and move on a curved line past the sun?

EDMOND HALLEY

Born in 1656 just outside London, Edmond Halley began his career in astronomy at a very early age. Because of his excellent work he became a Fellow of the Royal Society. However, it is because of his observations on and of comets that he has become a household name.

Edmond Halley 1656 – 1742.

In 1680 a fairly bright comet appeared in the sky and both Newton and Halley watched it. Halley was greatly interested in the phenomenon and decided to calculate its orbit. He discovered that the shape of its path matched very closely the shapes of several comet paths plotted in the past. Could they possibly be the paths of the same comet? If so, it meant that the same comet was capable of returning on the same path again and again. The orbits would therefore be elliptical not parabolic. The trouble was that at this time telescopes were so weak that only a small part of a comet's path could be tracked. In addition the difference between an elliptical and a parabolic curve was so small that astronomers could not tell the difference.

In 1682 another comet appeared. It was not quite as bright as that of 1680 but it was easily seen by the naked eye for some weeks. It reached perihelion on August 24th.

Halley later made calculations relating to its orbit. He assumed that the orbit was a parabola but again he saw similarities between this comet and two comets that had appeared in the past, those of 1607 and 1531. Perihelion distances were about the same and the direction of motion in both cases was retrograde, in other words, moving in the opposite direction to that of the earth on its orbit. Halley

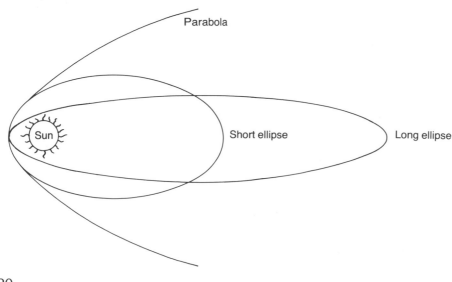

20

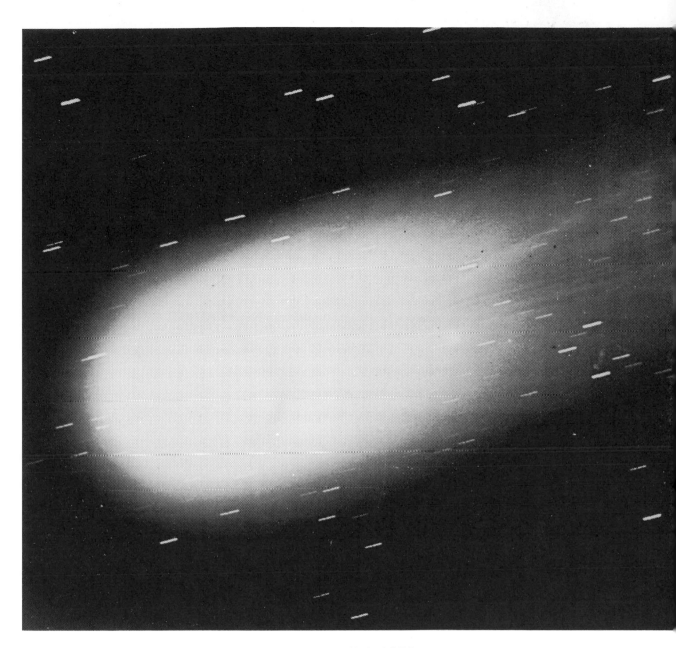

Halley's Comet photographed on its last visit in 1910.

searched again and found that comets seen in 1455, 1378 and 1301 also had similar orbits to that the 1682 comet. The time interval seemed to work out at about 76 years. So, in the year 1705 Halley predicted its return. The comet of 1682 would re-appear, he said, in 1758.

If Halley was right then the orbit of this particular comet would not be a parabola but an ellipse. He calculated that at one end of its elliptical orbit the comet would be 5,150,000,000 km (3,200,745,600 miles) from the sun while at the other end it would be only 87,000,000 km (54,070,851 miles) from the sun.

In 1742 Halley died. He had made the prediction . But it was up to others to prove that he was right.

21

HALLEY'S COMET

Halley knew that his 1758 prediction would not be exact. As it made its elliptical journey around the sun, the comet would be affected by the gravitational pull of large planets such as Jupiter and Saturn. He guessed that this would alter the comet's speed and so make it arrive back earlier or later than expected.

In 1757 Alexis Claude Clairant, another brilliant French mathematician, decided that he would calculate the exact amount of influence the planets in the solar system would have on the comet and so make a much more precise estimate of its time of arrival. Clairant worked night and day with two assistants for nearly six months until he had established that the comet would reach perihelion on April 13th 1759.

HALLEY CONFIRMED

In the meantime Charles Messier, working for Nicholas de l'Isle, astronomer of the French navy, was scanning the sky for anything that might resemble the comet. He used a very small telescope which he set up in the turret of the Hotel Cluny. De l'Isle had made some calculations of his own regarding the position the comet would be in as it

Herschel's ground telescope.

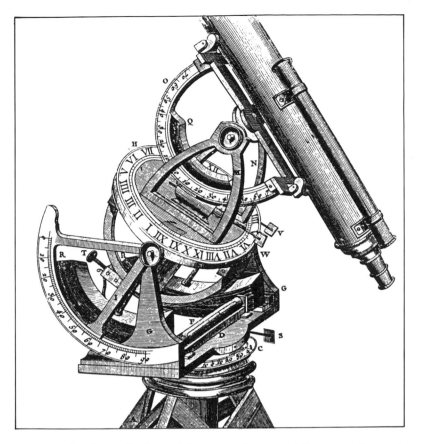

Nairn's equatorial telescope c1760.

approached perihelion. Messier observed for months with no success. But then on January 21, 1759 at about six o'clock in the evening he observed a faint glow. It was the comet!

Messier's discovery was not the first one. On Christmas night 1758, Johann Palitzsch, a Saxon astronomer, saw the comet and announced it straight away. His observation was quickly confirmed by other German astronomers.

Messier continued to watch for comets for the rest of his life and he observed over a dozen; however he is best known for the catalogue of star clusters and nebulae that he drew up. He produced this catalogue so that the clusters would not be mistaken for comets when observed by himself or other astronomers.

Comets are normally named for the person who discovers them but sometimes this honour goes instead to the mathematician who calculates its orbit. The comet of 1682 and 1759 was, of course, named after the man who successfully predicted its return, Edmond Halley.

Comets that return are called periodic comets, and those that complete their full orbit in less than 200 years are called short period comets. Astronomers prefix their names with a P, so Halley's comet is now known as Comet P/Halley.

SOME FAMOUS APPARITIONS

As we have seen, sightings of comets have been pretty fully recorded throughout the history of astronomy. Therefore it is not hard to imagine that many of the sightings were of the comet that returned in 1959, Halley's Comet. And once astronomers and historians knew just how many years it took Halley's Comet to travel around its orbital path, they were able to start looking for evidence to pinpoint sightings throughout history.

In 1852 John Russel Hird, an English astronomer, documented each return of the comet as far back as 12 BC. That was a long way back, but today we can trace it even further back to possible Chinese sightings of 240 BC.

In 1984 a group of scientists discovered references to Halley's comet on some Babylonian tablets in the British Museum. They were extremely excited about their find because the tablets recorded the return in 164 BC, a return that is not documented anywhere else in the world. They also mention the 67 BC return. This discovery, apart from filling in a time gap in Halley history, also demonstrates how accurate the records of the Babylonian astronomers were.

THE STAR OF BETHLEHEM

Some returns have created more interest for astronomers than others, and one of the most fascinating is that of 12 BC. This is the one that many people believe is related to the Christian story of the Star of Bethlehem. Could the moving star of Bethlehem have been Halley's Comet? When two planets are observed so closely together that they seem to be one, they are said to be in conjunction. The Star of Bethlehem was most likely a conjunction of Saturn and Jupiter. This happened three times in 7BC, and the conjunction on September 17th of that year, is probably the one that announced the birth of Christ.

MORE RECORDS!

The first recorded drawing of the comet was made in 1493 and shows a picture of the comet during its return of 684. It was supposed to have caused some very bad weather at the time!

The brightest-ever apparition was probably that of AD 837 although another very bright one occurred in AD 1301. This

The Babylonians recorded the appearance of Halley's Comet in 164BC on this cuneiform tablet. (Photographed by courtesy of British Museum)

time the comet was seen by an Italian painter called Giotto di Bondone. Giotto was asked to decorate the inside of a rich merchant's private chapel. This Giotto did and among the thirty eight scenes he painted was one called "The Adoration of the Magi". In the scene he painted the Star of Bethlehem as a comet. Giotto would be pleased to know that the British Aerospace Satellite which is being built to study the comet in 1985 is to bear his name.

The return of AD 1607 was the last one to be made in "pre-telescope" times. It was seen by Kepler and other noted astronomers of the time, and was described by one as a "flaming sword". Comets have been described as "sword-like" on a number of occasions and this may explain why they often seemed so fearsome.

The comet of 1835 was observed by John Herschel from near Cape Town in South Africa. John was the son of Sir William Herschel, the discoverer of the planet Uranus. Sir William had thought that Uranus was a comet at first until he realized he had made a far more important discovery!

Giotto's painting of the "Adoration of the Magi" showing Halley's Comet as he saw it in AD 1310.

COMETS LEAD TO...

Some people may think that observing comets is a pleasant pastime but that it is not as important as looking at grand things such as planets, galaxies or nebulae. But if we look very carefully at the history of comet observers and observations and astronomy generally, we can see that a rather curious pattern develops.

He proposes that the Earth is at the centre of the universe. The stars and planets are locked in a transparent 'spheres' above the Earth's atomosphere.

350-400 BC
Aristotle

He observes comets and suggests that they are pieces of Earth's atmosphere that have caught fire.

He states that the sun seems to have some influence on the way in which bodies move in space.

16th Century AD
Fracastoro

He observes that comet tails change direction as the comet moves, always pointing away from the sun.

Tycho believes that Aristotle's theories are not valid.

1543 –1601
Tycho Brahe

Tycho uses parallax to prove that comets are not part of the atmosphere but in the 'heavens' beyond. He says comets move through Aristotle's 'spheres'.

Copernicus states that the planets orbit the sun. Kepler confirms his theory and shows that the planets move in ellipses, not circles, around the sun.

1609 Nicolaus
Copernicus &
Johannes
Kepler

Kepler uses the straight line theory of cometary motion to show that Copernicus's theory works. He does not prove that comets have elliptical orbits.

Herschel discovers Uranus.

1781 William Herschel

Herschel believes that he is observing a comet, but the body turns out to be the 7th planet of the solar system.

He draws up an important catalogue of stars and nebulae.

1759–1781 Messier

Messier is a devoted observer of comets. His catalogue will prevent comets being mistaken for star clusters.

Newton solves the problem of universal gravity and publishes 'Principia'.

1687 Isaac Newton & Edmond Halley

Newton helps Halley solve the problem of comets and their motion which is linked to gravity. Halley goes on to predict a comet's orbit.

The work on orbits continues.

1664 Borelli

Borelli decides that comets move along parabolic paths.

Astronomers are intrigued by the questions of how the universe was formed.

1986

Comets are found to contain matter which scientists think is amongst the oldest in the world. 'Giotto' and the other space probes may provide some of the answers when they encounter Comet P Halley 1986.

Throughout the history of astronomy, whenever a great leap forward in understanding has been made, it has usually been closely linked to the study of comets. In the chart below you can see how the two aspects of astronomy link up.

OBSERVING HALLEY'S COMET WITH THE NAKED EYE

Any scientific expedition or project requires careful preparation if it is to be successful. If you are to make the most of this once-in-a-lifetime opportunity of observing Halley's Comet, you must make careful preparation some time before the comet is visible to the naked eye. First you have to learn something about how astronomers set about making their observations. Then you should make and prepare some simple equipment and, when the time comes, use the equipment to make your observations. Finally keep a careful record of your own observations and a scrap-book of newspaper cuttings and other material that you may collect during this time.

HEAVENLY ADDRESSES

Before the postman can deliver a letter he must know the address of the house of the person to whom the letter is addressed. Astronomers use special heavenly addresses so that they know where to point their telescopes if they want to study a particular object. There are a few ways of doing this. One way is to say how high (in degrees) the object is above the horizon and to give the angle (in degrees) which the object makes with either the north or south points. The first quantity is called the altitude of the object, and the other is called the azimuth. One set of observations you could make is to record the altitude and azimuth of Halley's Comet for different days and times. Besides a clock and a calendar you will also need a special device called an alt-azimuth instrument.

WHAT TO DO:

1. The sights are made by twisting two loops into a piece of wire as shown in fig 1.1. The loops should be at right-angles to the length of the wire. The cross-wires are made by glueing bits of cotton to the loops and then trimming them with a pair of scissors.

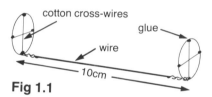

cotton cross-wires
glue
wire
10cm

Fig 1.1

2. Drill a small hole just big enough to take shaft of drawing pin in the semi-circular protractor at the point where all the lines meet.

3. Attach sights to protractor along its straight edge with sellotape (see fig 1.2a).

4. Attach protractor to top of batten with drawing pin so that it moves easily but not too freely about shaft of pin (see fig 1.2a).

5. Make a pointer on batten just below 0° point on protractor when exactly horizontal.

6. Make a marker 4.5 cm (⅛ in) long out of card and glue to base of batten.

7. Make a plumbline with cotton and small weight and fix this to opposite side of batten from protractor with sewing pin (see fig 1.2b).

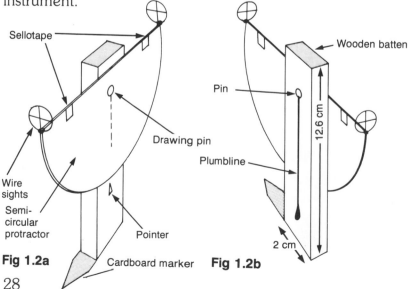

Sellotape

Wooden batten

Pin

12.6 cm

Drawing pin

Plumbline

Wire sights

Semi-circular protractor

Pointer

2 cm

Fig 1.2a

Cardboard marker

Fig 1.2b

MAKING AN ALT-AZIMUTH INSTRUMENT

You will need: Circular protractor 10 cm (4 in) diameter; semi-circular protractor 10 cm (4 in) diameter, wooden batten 2 cm x 2 cm x 12.6 cm (⅘ in x ⅘ in x 5 in); another piece of wood 15 cm x 15 cm x 1.2 cm (6 in x 6 in x 1½ in); drill; stiff card; four 6 mm (⅕ in) screws; two drawing pins, strong cotton; small weight; sewing pin; sellotape; wire; scissors; glue.

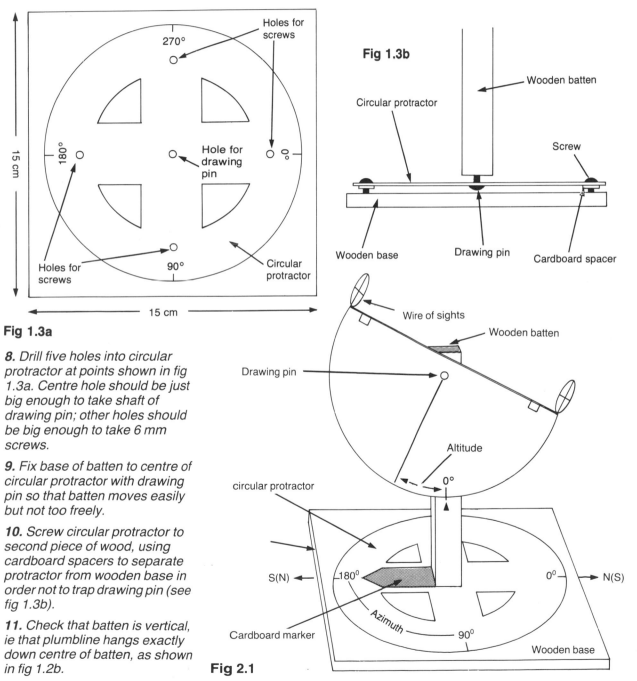

Fig 1.3a

Fig 1.3b

8. Drill five holes into circular protractor at points shown in fig 1.3a. Centre hole should be just big enough to take shaft of drawing pin; other holes should be big enough to take 6 mm screws.

9. Fix base of batten to centre of circular protractor with drawing pin so that batten moves easily but not too freely.

10. Screw circular protractor to second piece of wood, using cardboard spacers to separate protractor from wooden base in order not to trap drawing pin (see fig 1.3b).

11. Check that batten is vertical, ie that plumbline hangs exactly down centre of batten, as shown in fig 1.2b.

Fig 2.1

Before any astronomical instrument can be used effectively it has to be set up properly. In all cases this means it has to be properly positioned with respect to the directions north, south, east and west. To do this you first have to find the directions. A magnetic compass would give you the direction of magnetic north, but it is true north that is needed for the purpose of astronomical observations. One way of finding true north is to make a series of observations on the Sun.

You will need: A level, tiled or cemented surface in a sunny position out-of-doors, on which a 2 metre square (approx 2 yards) can be marked; a thin, straight piece of bamboo or other stick about 50 cm (20 in) long; a small flowerpot filled with soil (make sure the base is flat); a spirit level; steel tape-measure; graph paper; watch; protractor; chalk or pencil; string.

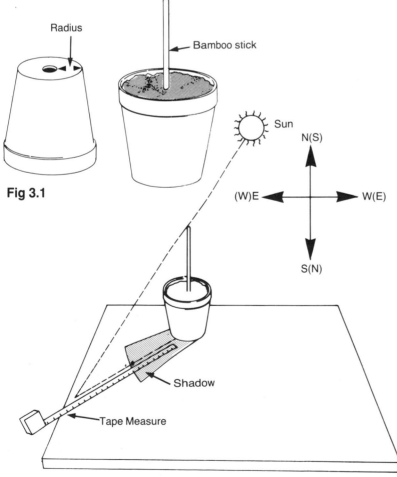

Fig 3.1

Fig 3.2   (The letters in brackets are for southern hemisphere observations)

Day 1: Today you will measure the changing length of the shadow cast by the Sun of the bamboo stick.

1. Measure and note the radius of the flowerpot base.

2. Put stick in centre of flowerpot and make sure it is absolutely vertical using the spirit level as a guide (see fig 3.1).

3. You should have a rough idea of the East-West and North-South directions. Mark out a 2 m square (approx 2 yards) on the level surface so that the edges are running approximately North-South and East-West. Place flowerpot midway along southernmost edge of area (see fig 3.2).

4. Starting at about 9.00 am measure length of shadow of stick at hourly intervals. Measure along the shadow from the base of the flowerpot as shown in fig 3.2. Always add the radius of the flowerpot base to your measurements.

5. Plot your results on the graph paper using 1 square to represent 1 cm (½ in) of shadow length (see fig 3.3). You will notice from your graph that the shadow length first decreases until about 12 noon and then increases again in the afternoon.

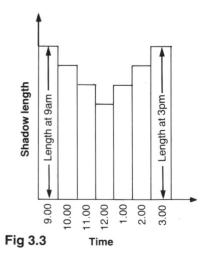

Fig 3.3   **Time**

Fig. 3.4a

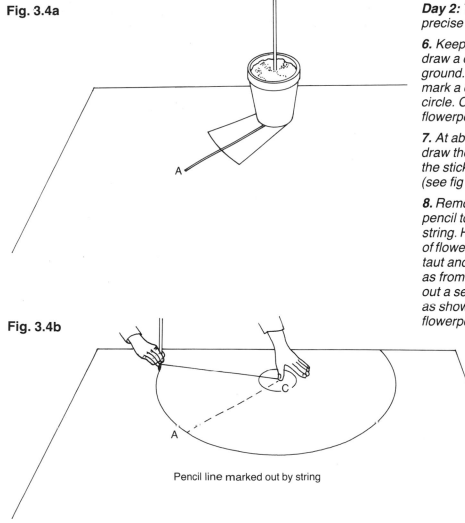

Day 2: Today you will find the precise North-South line.

6. Keeping flowerpot in position, draw a circle round base on the ground. Remove flowerpot and mark a dot in the centre of this circle. Call the dot C. Replace flowerpot.

7. At about 11 am measure and draw the line of shadow cast by the stick. Call the tip of this line A (see fig 3.4a).

8. Remove flowerpot. Tie chalk or pencil to one end of a piece of string. Hold string on centre mark of flowerpot circle. Keeping string taut and exactly the same length as from point A to point C, mark out a semi-circle on the ground, as shown in fig 3.4b. Replace flowerpot.

Fig. 3.4b

Pencil line marked out by string

Fig. 3.4c

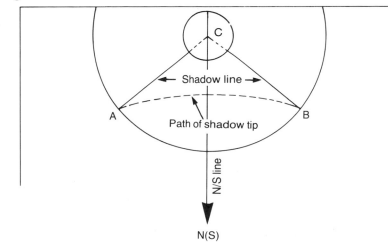

9. You will notice the shadow getting shorter towards noon and then lengthening again. Watch the shadow until it once again touches the semi-circle you have drawn. Draw in this shadow line and call the point where the tip touches the circle point B.

10. Remove flowerpot, and extend the two lines until they meet at C.

11. Bisect the angle ACB with your protractor. This line is pointing due North and South (fig 3.4c).

31

Since Halley's Comet only becomes visible to the naked eye late in 1985 you can get plenty of practice observing stars and planets beforehand.

Place the alt-azimuth on a level surface with the 0 mark on the circular protractor pointing towards north and the 180 mark towards south. For your first experiment choose a star close to the east in the early evening, making observations every half hour, as follows.

Keeping the base firm turn batten round and move protractor up or down until you can see your chosen star through the sights. The altitude is measured on the semi-circular protractor and the azimuth on the circular protractor (see fig 4.1). The azimuth angle is the angle between the marker and either the north or south points, depending on which way you are looking.

When using your instrument on the comet it is best to make a series of observations just after sunset on a number of days, in fact whenever the weather permits. From this you will be able to draw a diagram similar to those shown in figs 4.2 and 4.3.

Fig 4.1

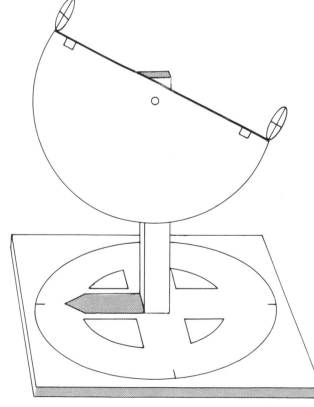

An alt-azimuth set up to observe Halley's Comet.

RECORD YOUR LATITUDE

The altitude and azimuth of any object in the sky depends, among other things, on the latitude of the place from which you are observing. In other words it depends on your distance from the equator in degrees. If your results are to be a proper scientific record, you should record your latitude on any charts or graphs you make. This can be found by looking up the latitude of your town, city or village in an atlas.

These charts show the height of Halley's Comet above the horizon in degrees (elevation) and the angle it makes with the north point (azimuth). This is measured in degrees from West to East at different times of the year and for two latitudes. These graphs show the estimated position of Halley's Comet in the northern hemisphere (top) and the southern hemisphere (bottom).

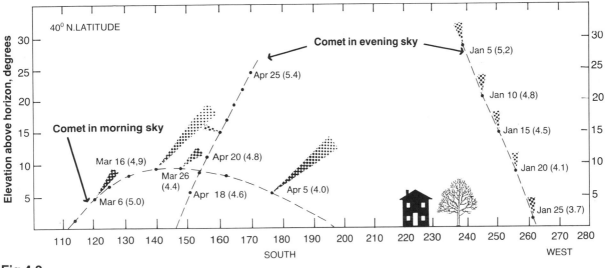

Fig 4.2

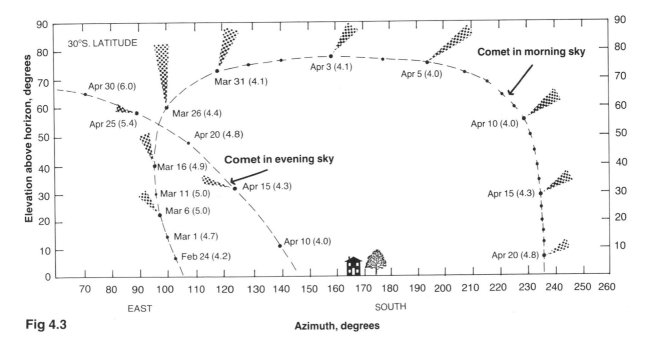

Fig 4.3

STAR MAPS

We have already learned about one method of finding the position of an object in the sky. There is another method which could well be called the Treasure Map Method. The position of a treasure is usually given, for example, in terms of so many paces from a tree stump, so many paces from an old headstone and so many paces from a gate. Astronomers use a similar method to pinpoint the positions of objects like planets, comets and the Moon in terms of how far they are from certain well known stars, or in which constellation they are to be found. However, before you can use this method you must be able to use a star map and you must be able to identify some well known constellations.

STAR MAPS AND GLOBES

Although the distances to the stars vary a great deal, it is possible to imagine that they are all fixed to a vast sphere, which is called the celestial sphere. For hundreds of years

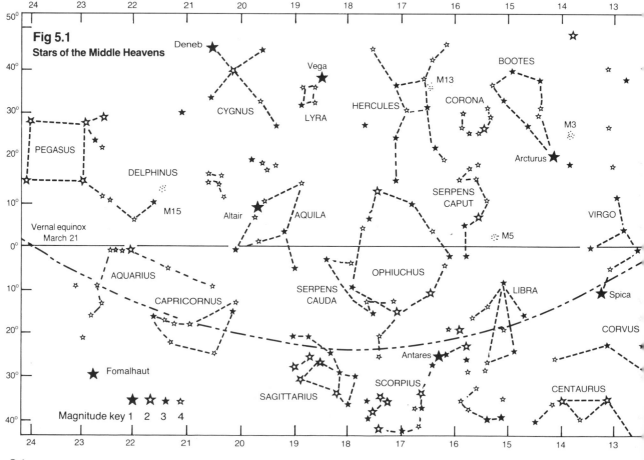

Fig 5.1
Stars of the Middle Heavens

astronomers have represented this sphere by means of a globe with the positions of the stars, and the outlines of the constellations plotted on this globe, in much the same way as the continents are plotted on a terrestrial globe. However, it is not convenient to carry such a celestial globe around with one, so celestial maps, or star maps, were invented.

In the maps we will use, the region near the north and south poles of the sky will be shown as discs, and the region near the equator of the sky will be seen as a cylinder which has been unrolled to form a rectangle (see figs 5.1,5.2,5.3).

The stars have been linked together to form imaginary shapes and patterns which the ancient astronomers named after animals or birds they saw in the countryside, or after their heroes or gods. Although the stars forming these shapes move across the sky as the Earth spins on its own axis, they do not seem to us to change their distances from each other over very long periods of time. These shapes are called the constellations.

Stars vary in brightness, so astronomers call the brightest stars magnitude 0, and the faintest stars that can be seen without a telescope are called magnitude 6. In our star maps

The ecliptic is the apparent pathway of the Sun against a stellar background. You can see it marked as a wavy line on the chart.

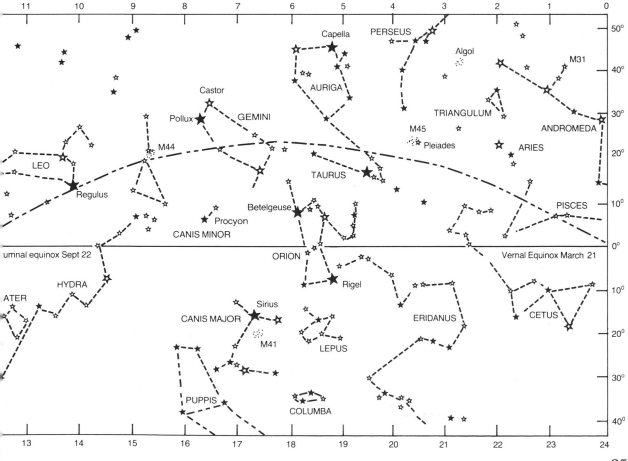

Northern Hemisphere Constellations

1 Cetus
2 Pisces
3 Aries
4 Triangulum
5 Andromeda
6 Pegasus
7 Lacerta
8 Cygnus
9 Equuleus
10 Delphinus
11 Aquila
12 Sagitta
13 Lyra
14 Draco
15 Hercules

16 Ophiucus
17 Serpens Caput
18 Corona Borealis
19 Bootes
20 Coma Berenices
21 Virgo
22 Canes Venatici
23 The Little Bear
24 Cepheus
25 Cassiopeia
26 Camelopardus
27 The Great Bear
28 Leo Minor
29 Leo
30 Lynx

31 Cancer
32 Hydra
33 The Little Dog
34 Gemini
35 Orion
36 Taurus
37 Auriga
38 Perseus

Fig 5.2

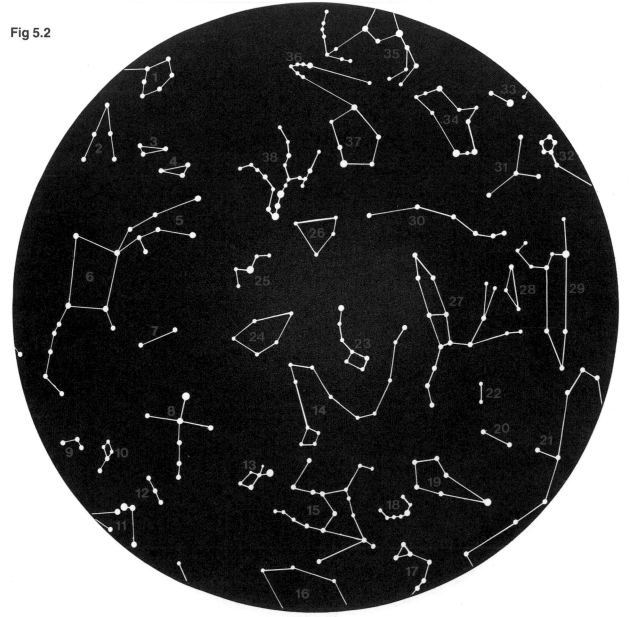

Southern Hemisphere Constellations

1 Capricornus
2 Aquarius
3 Pisces
4 Grus
5 Tucana
6 Phoenix
7 Sculptor
8 Cetus
9 Fornax
10 Eridanus
11 Lepus
12 Orion
13 Monoceros
14 Canis Major
15 Columba

16 Doradus
17 Pictor
18 Volans
19 Corina
20 Puppis
21 Pyxis
22 Antlia
23 Sextans
24 Crater
25 Hydra
26 Corvus
27 Virgo
28 Libra
29 The Serpent Holder
30 The Serpent

31 Aquila
32 Sagittarius
33 Corona
34 Scorpio
35 Lepus
36 Centaurus
37 The Australian Triangle
38 Ara
39 Telescopium
40 Pavo
41 Apus
42 Octans
43 Chamaeleon
44 Musca
45 The Southern Cross (Crux)

Fig 5.3

we only give positions of stars between 0 and 4 magnitudes. In using star maps to find your way around the sky it is best to start with the north polar constellation if you live in the northern hemisphere and with the south polar constellations if you live in the southern hemisphere.

The best known constellation in the northern polar region is often known as The Plough (fig 5.4). However it is sometimes called The Wagon; in America it is known as the Big Dipper and often it is linked with some fainter stars to form the Great Bear or Ursa Major. Two of the stars of the Plough are called the pointers, because a straight line drawn through them and continued on would lead to the North Star.

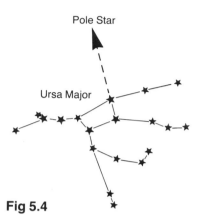

Fig 5.4

Having found The Plough, you can now use the star map of the north circumpolar stars, (circum – means around, – polar means the pole, so circumpolar means those stars that move around the pole of the sky) to find other well known constellations. A particularly easy one to pick out is the W shape of Cassiopeia. It will be found on the opposite side of the North Star from The Plough. Another fairly easy constellation to find, although it is rather faint, is the Little Bear or Ursa Minor. He is attached to the North Star by the tip of his tail.

HOW TO FIND HALLEY'S COMET

Although Halley's Comet will not be visible to the naked eye in November, during the middle of the month it can be seen with a pair of binoculars near to the Pleiades. This cluster of stars is in the constellation of Taurus the Bull, so it is a natural part of the sky in which to continue your project of getting to know the constellations.

The most convenient way of finding Taurus is to start with Orion the Hunter. The three stars that form the belt of Orion are very easy to identify as they are almost equally bright and in a straight line. These stars are sometimes called the Three Kings. If you extend the imaginary line joining these three stars out in one direction you will come to the brightest star in the sky - Sirius, or the dog star. It is so called because it is supposed to be in the head of Orion's larger dog, Canis Major. If you take your imaginary line out in the opposite direction, then you will come to a reddish star called Aldebaran, which is one of the eyes of Taurus the Bull.

An excellent way of re-inforcing your knowledge of the sky is to use a planisphere. In the next project we describe how to make and use a simple planisphere.

HOW TO MAKE A PLANISPHERE

A planisphere is used to find which constellations are visible on any night at any time of the year. Using the following instructions, make yourself a planisphere and then go out on a clear night to try it out. Note, a planisphere is not really a star map, but a device to help you find which constellations are visible on a particular night. It shows only the more important stars in each constellation and as a result, the shapes of the constellations differ slightly from those shown on the star maps. You will find that constellations are often drawn differently on different maps: do not worry about this because there is really no 'correct' way to draw any constellation.

You will need: Stiff white paper or thin card; acetate or celluloid sheet; brass paper fastener; glue.

Fig 6.1.

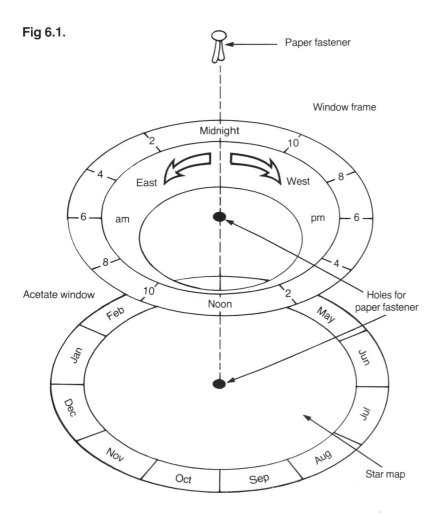

1. Trace star map shown in fig 6.2 (or fig 6.4 if you live in the Southern Hemisphere) onto stiff paper or thin card and cut out.

2. Trace circular window frame shown in fig 6.3 (or fig 6.5) on to white card and cut out. Carefully cut out shaded area.

3. Draw circle of same diameter as window frame onto acetate sheet and cut out.

4. Glue window frame to acetate circle to make window. Place window over top of star map so that centres coincide and with a sharp point make holes through centres of both. Join with brass paper fastener as shown in fig 6.1.

Plans for a Planisphere for the Northern Hemisphere

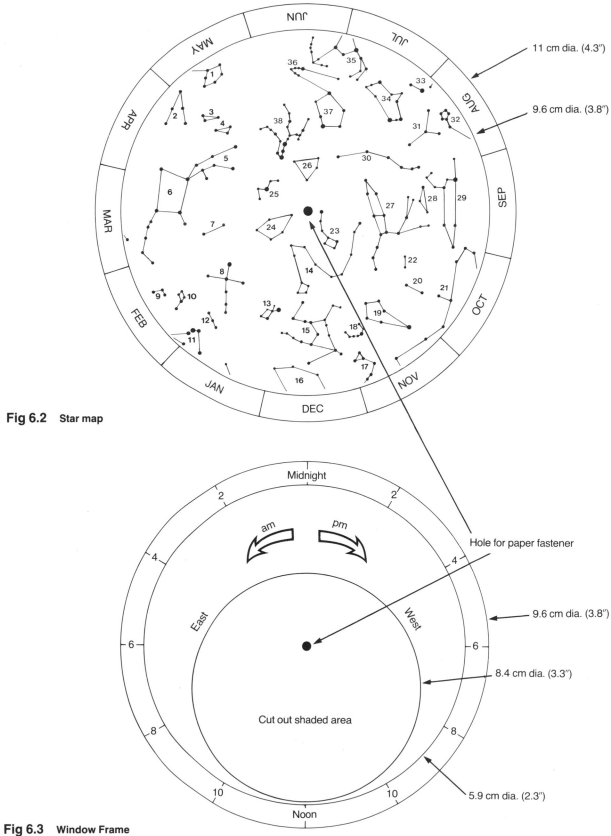

Fig 6.2 Star map

Fig 6.3 Window Frame

40

Plans for a Planisphere for the Southern Hemisphere

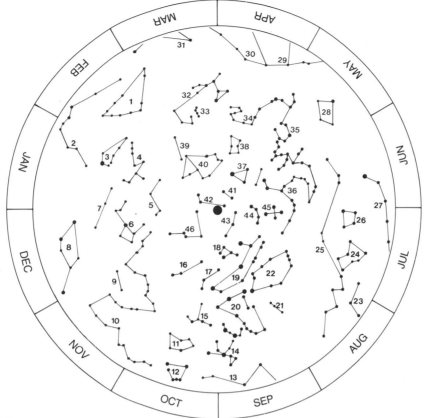

Fig 6.4   Star Map

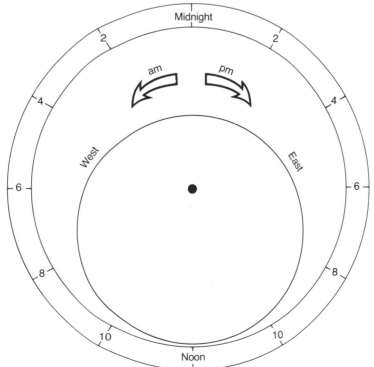

Fig 6.5   Window Frame

USING THE PLANISPHERE

To find which constellations are visible at a given time of night on a particular date, line up the time on the window frame with date on the star map (this will have to be an estimate since this planisphere is too small to show days of the month). The constellations visible that night will be those showing through the clear part of the window. To find the direction and position of stars in the real sky, hold the planisphere facing downwards above your head. If you live in the nothern hemisphere point the midnight mark towards the north and noon mark towards the south. If you live in the southern hemisphere point the midnight mark towards the south and the noon mark towards the north. The eastern and western horizons are marked at the edge of the clear window. The positions of the constellations on that part of the map which appears in the window will be very similar to their positions in the actual sky.

CHARTING THE PATH OF HALLEY'S COMET

Fig 7.1 shows the path of Halley's Comet through the constellations from November 1985 to May 1986. This is the predicted path based on calculations using the information obtained from all previous sightings of the comet. It is part of the astronomer's duty to check whether the comet will in fact follow the predicted path, and you can do your own checking. When the comet becomes visible to the naked eye you can use a simple device called a 'forestaff' to measure the angle which the head of the comet makes with certain well-known stars. You can then use these measurements to plot the position of the comet on a star map for a few different dates. You will then be able to see if it is really following its predicted path.

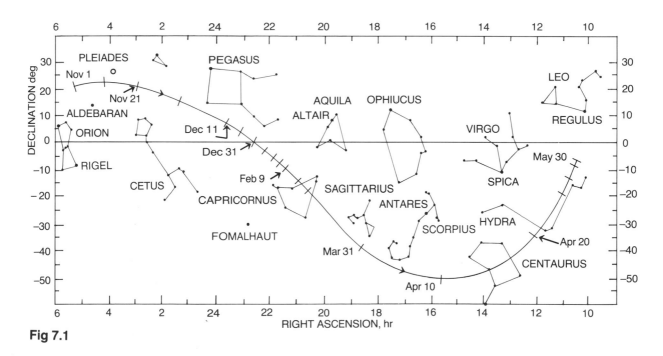

Fig 7.1

MAKING A FORESTAFF

You will need: A copy of the star map provided in Fig 5.1; a small table; torch; piece of red cloth; elastic band; two transparent plastic rulers about 30 cm (12 in) long; piece of wood 60 cm (24 in) long and about 2 cm diameter; No. 8 screw 1.5 cm (⅙ in) long; brace fitted with a No. 8 bit; drill; small nail and 200 cm (2¼ yards) of string.

Fig 7.2

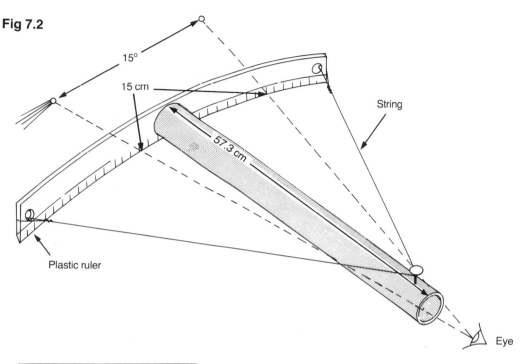

WHAT TO DO:

1. Drill three holes in one of the rulers. One at the centre and two near the ends.

2. Drill a hole in the end of the piece of wood, and screw the ruler to the wood as shown in fig 7.2.

3. Drive the small nail into the piece of wood 57.3 cm (22.5 in) from the end to which the ruler is attached.

4. Fasten one end of the length of string to one end of the ruler, using one of the holes you drilled, and after passing it around the nail fasten the other end of the string to the other end of the ruler. This should be done in such a way that each straight part of the string is 57.3 cm (22.5 in) long (see fig 7.2.). Each centimetre of ruler now makes an angle of one degree at the nail and the whole ruler can measure angles of up to 30 degrees.

5. Cover torch light with red cloth and hold in place with elastic band.

6. Set up the table outside on a clear night. Place the map on the table. The torch is to help you to see what you are doing without disturbing your view of the night sky.

7. All maps have a scale, stating how many centimetres/inches there are to a mile. The next thing you have to do is to find the scale of your star map. This can easily be done by measuring the distance between any two stars, close to the predicted path of the comet, using your forestaff, and then measuring the distance between the same two stars on the map using an ordinary ruler. From this you can find how many degrees in the actual sky are equal to so many centimetres/ inches on your star map.

8. Next measure the distances of the comet from three nearby stars and transfer the position of the comet on to your star map. Repeat this on several separate dates. Compare these positions with those shown in fig 7.1.

OBSERVING HALLEY'S COMET WITH A PAIR OF BINOCULARS

Binoculars are extremely useful for observing comets. Although they do not have the same magnification as a telescope they have a wider field of view than most telescopes. In mid November Halley's Comet will be visible with binoculars close to the cluster of stars called The Pleiades (sometimes known as the Seven Sisters), so you could in fact see it before it becomes visible to the naked eye.

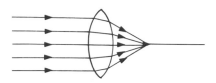

Light is collected by a converging lens.

Most of the lenses used in binoculars are the type called converging lenses. Each lens will therefore have two convex sides. A line drawn through the lens from edge to edge and passing trough its centre is called the "plane of the lens". A line which passes through the plane in the centre of the lens and at right angles to it, is called the "axis of the lens". When beams of light pass through the lens and are bent by it, they converge, or meet, at a particular point on the axis. This point is the focal point and the distance from lens to focal point is called the focal length. The front lenses in binoculars are called objectives. They have fairly long focal lengths. The eyepieces have much shorter focal lengths. Magnification is found by the ratio:

$$\frac{\text{focal length of objective}}{\text{focal length of eyepiece}}$$

Rays of light coming from an object run parallel to the axis of the lens. When they enter the lens they are bent. If the distance between object and lens is greater than the focal length the image of the object can be focused on a screen. The only drawback is that it is seen upside down (fig. 8.1). When the distance between object and lens is less than the focal length you cannot focus the image on a screen but you can look through the lens in the direction of the object and see a magnified one

Formation of images by a converging lens

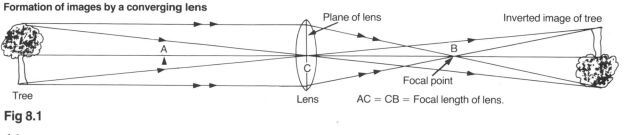

Plane of lens — Inverted image of tree

Tree — Lens — AC = CB = Focal length of lens. — Focal point

Fig 8.1

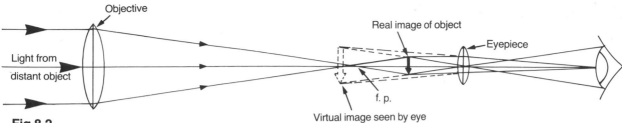

Fig 8.2

Binoculars combine both of these scientific "laws". In fact they use two sets of lenses, one in each scope. The front ones, called objective lenses, collect light and form an upside down image of the object on the inside of each scope. The lenses at the other end, called eyepieces, create a magnified image when you look through them (fig 8.2).

USING YOUR BINOCULARS

The main problem with using binoculars for astronomy is keeping them steady. Some observers mount their instruments on special adjustable mounts, but you can do just as well by using a comfortable armchair. Just hold the binoculars in both hands resting your elbows on the arms of the chair! It gives a steady, adjustable mount, and is comfortable if you want to observe for any length of time.

WARNING. NEVER LOOK AT THE SUN THROUGH BINOCULARS.

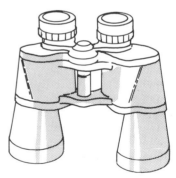

When observing Halley's Comet through a pair of binoculars there are three things you can do.

Appearance. First you could note its appearance. Does it have a tail? What is the relationship between the coma and the tail? Try to sketch, however roughly, what you see.

Position. When the comet is in the centre of the field of view, try to remember its relationship with respect to the other stars in the field of view, and record this in a sketch.

Magnitude. Astronomers try to estimate the magnitude of any object in the sky by comparing it with the known magnitudes of nearby stars. You can get these magnitudes from a star atlas or map. However, since a comet is not a star-like object, it is best to defocus your binoculars so that the stars in the field of view also have fuzzy appearances like the comet and then carry out the comparison of magnitudes.

PHOTOGRAPHING HALLEY'S COMET

The 1835 return of Halley's Comet missed the birth of astronomical photography by only five years. The first photograph of the Moon was taken by Henry Draper, Professor of Chemistry at the University of New York, in 1840, so astronomers had to wait for the 1910 return before they could photograph the comet for the first time.

Taking a good photograph of a comet through a telescope or with a camera is not an easy task. This is because Earth is spinning on its own axis, causing the stars to apparently move across the sky, and the comet is also moving with respect to the background. For long exposure times a complicated drive system is necessary for telescope and camera, which will allow one to 'drive' the telescope to keep track of the comet itself. However it is possible to take a reasonable photograph of Halley's Comet, when it becomes visible to the naked eye, with any camera that is able to take time exposures.

Halley's Comet photographed on its last visit in 1910. The moon is clearly visible at bottom left.

Halley's Comet of 1910 photographed early in its journey towards Earth.

WHAT YOU NEED

A camera able to take time exposures, a camera tripod, a cable release, a hat or cap, a watch and a fast film (Kodak 1000 ASA or Fuji 1600).

WHAT TO DO

Load the camera with the film. Set it up on the tripod with the lens pointing in the direction of the comet. Hold the cap over the lens, but without touching the camera, open the shutter with the cable release, remove the cap and after the required time (about a minute or so) cover the lens with the cap, and then close the shutter with the release. Doing it this way you avoid camera shudder.

With an exposure of about a minute star trails on the film will hardly be noticable. You will have to take several exposures, some less and some more than one minute, if you are to get a good image of the comet.

Remember to warn the people processing your film that you have been photographing Halley's Comet so that they will not discard the developed film if it does not have on it what they normally expect.

Normally when we think of telescopes and looking at the skies, we think of long tubes full of lenses and mirrors, like the one you see at your local observatory. Like binoculars, these telescopes capture light waves that are given off by the objects they are focused on. However, there are telescopes that do not record light waves at all. These are known as radio telescopes and they detect radio waves instead. Objects in space give off radio waves just as they give off light waves. And radio waves can give us a great deal of information about the objects from which they come.

Radio telescopes operate at wavelengths which are much shorter than those used for television. They can be from a few centimetres in length to about a metre. Radio astronomers often use a length of 21 cm (8¼ in) as this is broadcast by the most plentiful substance in the universe, hydrogen gas.

The radio dish telescope at Arecibo, Puerto Rico.

Radio waves are collected by the telescope's large round dish and then focused onto a detector, much like a lens focuses light waves. The detector is hooked in to an amplifier so that the energy produced is much stronger. Because radio waves are so much longer than light waves the collection dish must be very large, something with a diameter of as much as 100 metres (109.5 yards).

The Arecibo telescope in Puerto Rico is 305 metres (334 yards) in diameter. It is so big that unlike most dishes it cannot be "steered" or pointed in a particular direction. Instead it scans the sky as the earth rotates. The Arecibo is in fact a Radar telescope which means that it emits a pulse like a radar detecting device which is then received back at the dish after being reflected from an object. Using this method it could give valuable data on the size of a comet's coma or the size of its nucleus.

The radio telescope at Westerbork radio observatory in the Netherlands.

SPACE PROBES TO HALLEY'S COMET

Scientifically this visit of Halley's Comet will differ from all other visits in one very important respect. For the first time the comet can be investigated by the methods of space science. Space science differs from astronomy in that astronomers use ground based telescopes and instruments, whereas space scientists use laboratory-type instruments and special cameras on board space-craft. Six space-craft will be visiting the neighbourhood of the comet and they will give us more information about its physical nature than we could ever hope to get from ground based instruments alone. What is more, much of this information will be transmitted over radio and television, and there will be special newspaper reports. You can combine all this information with your own ground based observations, just as astronomers, both professional and amateur, will be doing all over the world.

SATELLITES

If you had to throw a stone from the top of a mountain it would curve gently down before striking the ground. You will know by now that it is force of gravity which causes it to do this. The harder and faster you throw the stone the further it will go. You could imagine a situation in which you threw the stone so hard that it went into orbit around the Earth. This is in fact the principle behind the satellite (see fig 9.1).

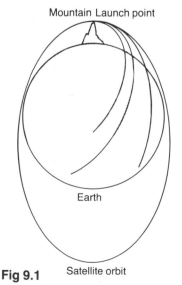

Mountain Launch point

Earth

Fig 9.1 Satellite orbit

Giotto, the European Space Agency probe will cross the tail of Halley's Comet in March 1986. Ten different experiments on board will send back valuable information on the comet.

SPACE PROBES

Just as a man-made satellite is really an artificial moon, so a space probe is really an artificial planet fitted with special instruments. When a space probe is launched from Earth it is put into orbit around the Sun in such a way that it will cross the orbit of another body in the Solar System.

Since the probe is launched from one moving body to another, the time of launching must be such that the orbits of the probe and the other body will cross at exactly the desired meeting place (see fig 9.2).

The motor of the rocket that launches the probe is only

The Launch of the Voyager space probes towards Jupiter is typical of this kind of planned orbit.

E1 and J1 represent the ideal positions of Earth and Jupiter at the time of the launch. E2 and J2 represent the positions of Earth and Jupiter when the probe reaches Jupiter. The arrow spiralling out from the centre represents the total angle covered by Earth, ie, 2.73 Earth years have elapsed.

Fig 9.2

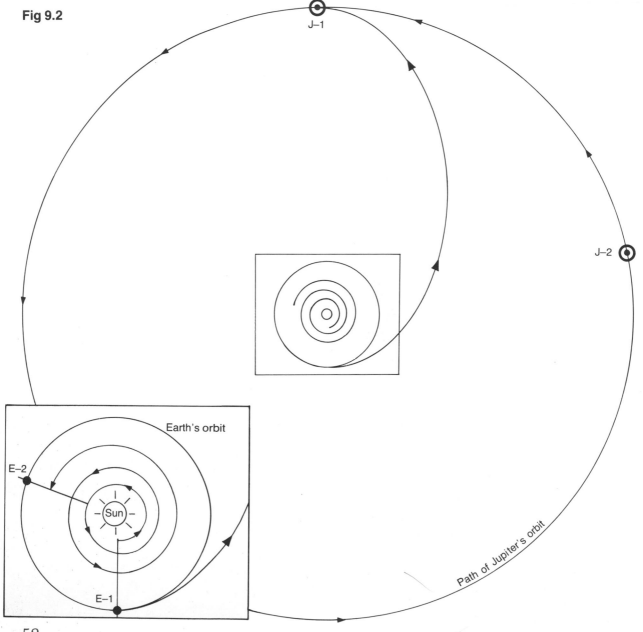

Fig 9.3

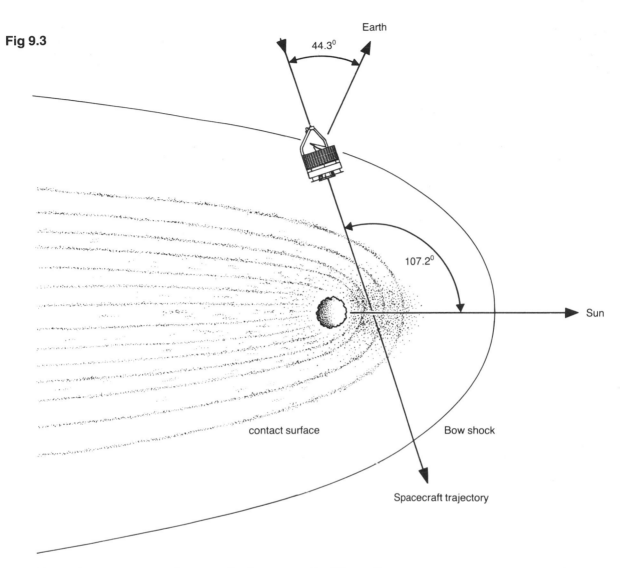

Earth

44.3°

107.2°

Sun

contact surface

Bow shock

Spacecraft trajectory

used for a short time, in what is called a controlled "burn", to put the probe into its required orbit. This orbit will of course be different from that of Earth. In principle it is not necessary to use the rocket motor again unless a further short "burn" is required to put the probe into the same orbit as the other body. So we see that for most of its orbit the probe is just moving under the force of gravity, and its own momentum.

The meeting of Halley's Comet and Giotto will undoubtedly end in the destruction of the space–probe.

GIOTTO

Halley's Comet is moving around the Sun in the opposite direction to the planets. Also, its orbit is inclined to that of Earth by almost 18 degrees. For these reasons Giotto, the space-probe of the E.S.A. (see fig 9.3), will be launched in July into an orbit that will take it across the path of the comet just as the comet crosses the plane of the Earth's orbit. This will occur in March 1986.

Make an orbital model: This will show the relative positions of Earth, Giotto and Halley's Comet at various important stages of their orbits.

You will need: Sheet of white card approx 20 cm square (8 in); strip of acetate approx 16 cm x 6 cm (6¼ in x 2¼ in); strong glue; scissors; pieces of stiff card for wedges; pen and red felt pen.

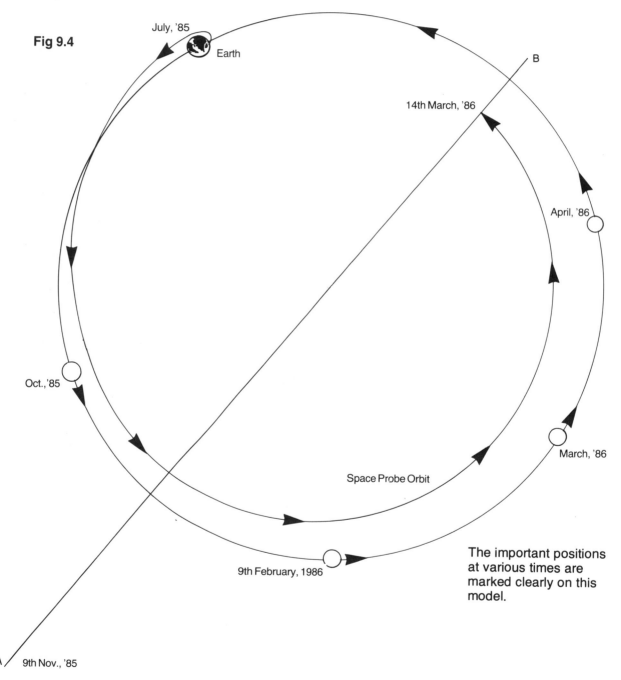

Fig 9.4

July, '85

Earth

B

14th March, '86

April, '86

Oct., '85

March, '86

Space Probe Orbit

9th February, 1986

The important positions at various times are marked clearly on this model.

A   9th Nov., '85

1. Trace the orbits of Earth and Giotto onto the sheet of stiff card (fig 9.4).

2. Trace the orbit of Halley's Comet onto the strip of acetate (fig 9.5).

3. Sellotape the lower edge of the acetate strip to the card, matching A and B on the strip to A and B on the card.

4. Make two triangular wedges having an angle of 18 degrees using very stiff card. Each wedge should have 2 tabs A and B as shown on fig 9.6. Glue tab A to the base card and tab B to the acetate strip.

Fig 9.5

B

A

The orbit of Halley's Comet lies at an angle of 18° from that of Giotto.

The curve representing Halley's orbit will now make an angle of 18° with the orbit of Earth.

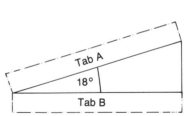

Tab A

18°

Tab B

Tab A

18°

Tab B

Fig 9.6

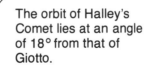

The construction of the main parts of Giotto are clearly shown in fig 9.7. The boost motor and the fuel tanks are on the right of the diagram. At the bottom, just right of centre, can be seen one of the shell segments used to cover the boost motor after it has been fired. The high gain dish antenna is an aerial used to transmit and receive radio waves to and from the Earth and space-craft respectively.

Just as a toy top is kept stable by its spinning, so Giotto will be stablized by spinning about an axis down the middle of the craft. However the high gain dish antenna has to point towards Earth, so it is fitted with a de-spin mechanism which will keep it pointing in the right direction although the craft is spinning. The solar cel array uses solar radiation energy to power the equipment on board.

When the craft encounters the comet, dust particules will strike the lower end at speeds 50 times greater than the speed of a bullet. To protect the craft during encounter a special dust protection shield is fitted. This shield consists of two parts. The first part consists of a rather thin bumper shield, about 1 mm (.04 in) thick, and the second part, behind the bumper shield, consists of a more massive rear shield 13.5 mm (½ in) thick. The bumper shield vaporises the particles striking it and the cloud of vapour produced spreads out in the space separating the shields, so the effect is absorbed over a larger area.

The ten experiments on board will study different parts of the comet. However these experiments can be divided into four main groups. The first group will study the nature of the dust including the sizes, masses and chemicals of which the particles are made. These experiments will also look at how the dust is distributed in space around the coma.

The next set of experiments will investigate the atoms of different chemicals which are present in the gases of the coma. One experiment will measure the masses of neutral atoms and the other will measure the masses of charged (or ionized) atoms.

The third group contains one important instrument - the colour camera. With this camera it is hoped that it will be possible to take colour photographs of the nucleus.

One important set of experiments is concerned with the plasma of the comet. A plasma consists of charged atoms (or ions). and as a result of their electric charges these ions will interact with magnetic fields. The Sun has a magnetic field which is similar in some ways to the magnetic field of the Earth. As we have seen, a stream of very fast moving particles comes to us from the Sun, called the Solar Wind.

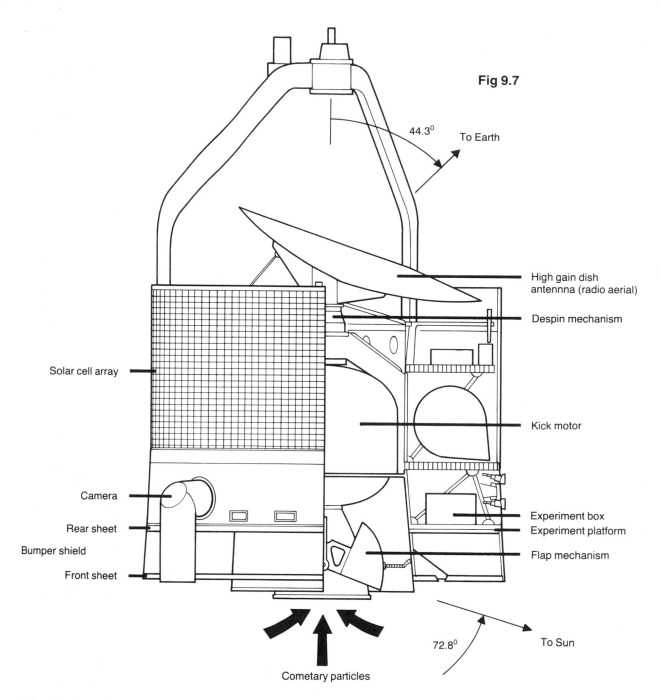

Fig 9.7

44.3° To Earth

High gain dish antennna (radio aerial)

Despin mechanism

Solar cell array

Kick motor

Camera

Experiment box
Experiment platform

Rear sheet

Bumper shield

Flap mechanism

Front sheet

72.8° To Sun

Cometary particles

This wind carries part of the magnetic field of the Sun with it. The plasma of the comet will interact, not only with the wind, but also with the magnetic field within the wind. This last set of experiments will investigate how the cometary plasma interacts with the Solar Wind and with this magnetic field (called the Interplanetary Magnetic Field).

VEGA 1 AND 29

The Russians have already launched two space probes to encounter Halley's Comet - Vega 1 and 2. Both probes consist of two parts of a Venus probe and a comet flyby component. The Venus probes will separate from the other components before the encounter with Venus. Each probe will consist of two parts; a balloon which will be released into the atmosphere of Venus, and a soft-lander which will collect and analyse soil samples. Each comet flyby component will get a gravitational tug from Venus as it swings around the planet and this will help boost its speed as it continues on its journey to the comet. These probes will carry similar experiments to those on Giotto - including wide and narrow-angle cameras. Both these probes will encounter the comet before Giotto, although their approaches will not be as close. The information they collect will be passed to the European Space Agency so that Giotto can be more precisely guided as it approaches Halley's Comet.

PLANET A AND MS–T5

The Japanese are also launching two space probes to the comet. The first probe, MS–T5, will really be a test probe, but it will carry out some experiments. The second probe, Planet A, will reach the comet about the same time as the first, which was launched eight months earlier. The two most important experiments on Planet A, are a camera and a device for measuring the particles in the solar wind.

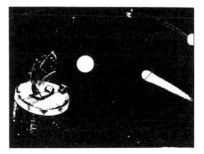

THE NASA CONTRIBUTION

The National Aeronautics and Space Agency in America were not given sufficient funds to launch their own purpose designed Halley's Comet project. Instead they are improvising by using three different probes already launched for other purposes to carry out some investigations on the comet. Because they were not purpose built for such investigations they do not have the necessary protective shields to prevent damage to the probes from cometary dust particles, so they will carry out their studies from a safe distance.

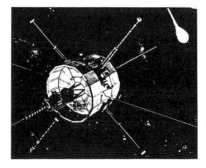

FOLLOW UP YOUR INTERESTS

If Halley's Comet has aroused your interest in astronomy, you might like to take the subject up as a hobby. Below we suggest some ways you could do this.

JOINING A CLUB OR SOCIETY

Many villages, towns and cities all over the world have their own local astronomy societies. The best source for clubs and societies in your areas is your local library.

Federation of Astronomical Societies
Most amateur societies in the UK belong to the Federation. You can find out about the society in your area from the Handbook for Astronomical Societies, published by the Federation and available from Mr Brian Jones, 47 St Blaise Court, Off Manchester Road, Bradford, West Yorkshire BD5 0QE.

Junior Astronomical Society
This is the best national society for a beginner to join since it caters for beginners of all ages, and publishes a very good quarterly magazine on popular astronomy, as well as distributing circulars containing much useful information. Details from Ms Barbara Kern, Enrolment Secretary, 22 Queensthorpe Road, Sydenham, London SE26 4PH.

Other useful societies
British Astronomical Association (for serious amateurs)
Burlington House, Piccadilly, London W1V 0NL.

Royal Astronomical Society (largely for professional astronomers)
Burlington House, Piccadilly, London W1V 0NL. Tel: 01-734 4582

Association for Astronomy Education (largely for schoolteachers)
Secretary: Capt. P Richards-Jones, London Schools Planetarium, Wandsworth School, Sutherland Grove, London SW18.

Astronomical Society of Australia
c/o Astronomy Department, University of Sydney, Sydney, NSW, Australia 2006. Tel: 02 6922680.

The Astronomical Society of Southern Africa
c/o The South African Astronomical Observatory, PO Box 9, Observatory, Cape Town, 7935 South Africa. Tel: 021 470025.

The Royal Astronomical Society of New Zealand, Inc.
PO Box 3181, Wellington, New Zealand. Tel: 04 677661.

Canadian Astronomical Society
Dominion Astrophysical Observatory, Victoria, British Columbia V8X 4M6. Tel: 604 3883975.

NASA
John F Kennedy Space Center, Florida 32899, USA.

PRACTICAL ACTIVITIES

Since astronomy is an observational science, practical activities are very important. A book of projects for the beginner in astronomy is *Adventures with Astronomy* by Percy Seymour, published by John Murray (1983) and available from bookshops, price £4.25. Although originally intended for people living in the northern hemisphere, all but three of the 22 projects can be carried out equally well in the southern hemisphere. Of the three remaining projects, two have been modified for use all over the world as detailed earlier in this book.

Another book along practical lines is *Exploring The Heavens* by D V Clish, obtainable from Glenmore Publications, 2 Woodland Road, Exeter, Devon, price £2.95. There is an activity pack to accompany this book, price £2.95.

Home computers offer an exciting range of astronomy activities. There are several programs available from computer stores for teaching yourself some basic astronomy via the computer graphics of your micro. *Halley's Comet* by Donald Tattersfield (Basil Blackwell, 1985) has a collection of programs for calculating the position of the comet in the sky and with respect to Earth. Cassettes of these programs are available for Spectrum and BBC Model B. *ZX Spectrum Astronomy* by Maurice Gavin (Sunshine Books, 1984) is a general collection of programs on astronomy for the Sinclair ZX Spectrum.

GLOSSARY

asteroid A word meaning "star–like": the term given to the small planetary bodies the majority of which orbit the Sun between Mars and Jupiter.

astronomical unit The mean distance of the Earth from the Sun, equal to 149,597,870 kilometres (92,955,807 miles).

azimuth Angular distance around the horizon, usually from north (0^0) round by east (90^0), south (180^0), and west (270^0).

celestial sphere The imaginary sphere which carries the stars and other celestial objects and is marked with lines of celestial latitude and longitude. It appears to rotate around the Earth once a day.

constellation One of the eighty–eight groups of stars into which the sky has been divided.

ellipse The geometrical shape obtained by running a pencil around inside a loop of string dropped over two pins. Each planet moves in an elliptical orbit.

ellipse The geometrical shape obtained by running a pencil around inside a loop of string dropped over two pins. Each planet moves in an elliptical orbit.

focal length The distance between the lens or mirror and the image it forms of an infinitely distant object.

focal point The place where the rays of light focused by a lens or mirror converge to form an image of the distant object observed.

galaxy A self–contained aggregation of stars and star–producing material (gas, dust).

latitude The distance in degrees of a point on a planet's surface, measured from the equator towards the north or south pole.

magnitude The brightness rather than the size of a celestial object.

nebula An interstellar cloud consisting mainly of hydrogen, but also containing small quantities of other elements.

objective A term applied to the main lens in a refracting telescope.

orbit The imaginary path traced out by an object moving through space under the gravitational control of another body.

parallax A shift in the apparent position of a body due to the motion of the observer.

perihelion The point on the orbit of a planetary body that is closest to the Sun.

quasar A "quasi-star" or "quasi stellar object". An extra–galactic energy source of enormous power and relatively small size.

reflector A general term describing any telescope that forms an image by using a mirror.

retrograde motion Orbital motion in a direction opposite to that in which all the major planets move.

INDEX

A

alt–azimuth 28,29,30,31,32,33
Arecibo telescope 49
Aristarchus 16
Aristotle 14,15,19,26
aster kometus 14
asteriod 8

B

Bayeux tapestry 5
binoculars 7,38,44,45
Borelli, Giovanni 18,19,26
Brahe, Tycho 14,15,27

C

Clairaut, Alexis Claude 22
coma 12,45,49,56
cometary cloud 9
comet pills 5
constellations 34,35,36,37,39,42
Copernicus – Nikolas 17

DEF

deferent 17
ellipse 16,17,18,20,21,22
epicycle 17
European Space Agency 59
forestaff 42

G

galaxy – elliptical 11
        – irregular 11
        – radio 11
        – spiral 10,11
Giotto 24,25,51,52,53,54,
        55,56,57,59
globes 3,5
gravity 8,18,19,22,50,53

H

Halley, Edmond 6,19,20,21,
        22,27
Herschel, John 25,27
Herschel, William 25

KL

Kepler, Johannes 17,19,26
latitude 33
lens 44,45,46,48

M

Messier, Charles 22
Milky Way 10,11
moons 8,9

N

Newton, Isaac 18,19,20,27
nucleus 12

O

observatory 48
Oort, Jan 9,11,26
orbit 6,9,14,17,19,20,21,52,
        53,54,55

PQR

parabopla 18,19,20,21
parallax 14,15
perihelion 6,7,20,22
photograph 46,47,56
planisphere 38,39,40,41,42
Pleiades 38,44
Plough, The 38
probes 50,51,52,53,54,55,59
quasar 11
radio telescope 48

S

satellites 50,51,52,53
Solar system 8,9,10,14,16,17,
        18,22,52
solar wind 58,59
spectroscopy 12
star map 38,39,40,41,42,45
Star of Bethlehem 24
Stonehenge 16

T

Tail – dust 12,13,45
        – plasma 12,13,56,58
telescope 7,20,22,23,28,36,
        44,48,49,50

ACKNOWLEDGEMENTS

The Publishers are most grateful to the following people, organisations and societies for their help in compiling this book:

Peter Hindley: Librarian, Royal Astronomical Society, Burlington House, London W1.

David Hughes: Senior Lecturer in Physics and Astronomy, University of Sheffield, for permission to reproduce his photo of the Giotto, 'Adoration of the Magi'.

Trevor Philip Ltd: 2, Prince Albert St, Brighton, Sussex, for permission to use the photo of the orrery reproduced on page 8.

The Royal Observatory, National Maritime Museum, Greenwich, London SE10, for their help in locating information and illustrative reference.

Mr D V Clish,   2, Woodland Rd, Exeter, Devon, for permission to reproduce the star maps on pages 34, 35.

John Murray (Publishers) Ltd,   50, Albemarle St, London W1, for kind permission to use material from their publication 'Adventures with Astronomy' on the activity pages 28, 29, 30, 31, 32, 36, 37 and 41 of this book.

British Aerospace, 100 Pall Mall, London SW1, for the pictures of the Giotto space probe on pages 50,51, 56,57

Jeremy Gower,   for the colour illustrations on pages 11 15,16,17

Gerry Bailey,   for his assistance with researching and compiling the first section of this book.